Traditional Soap Making Techniques Explained

A Guide to Making Homemade Soap

By: Esther Beckett

PUBLISHERS NOTES

Disclaimer

This publication is intended to provide helpful and informative material. It is not intended to diagnose, treat, cure, or prevent any health problem or condition, nor is intended to replace the advice of a physician. No action should be taken solely on the contents of this book. Always consult your physician or qualified health-care professional on any matters regarding your health and before adopting any suggestions in this book or drawing inferences from it.

The author and publisher specifically disclaim all responsibility for any liability, loss or risk, personal or otherwise, which is incurred as a consequence, directly or indirectly, from the use or application of any contents of this book.

Any and all product names referenced within this book are the trademarks of their respective owners. None of these owners have sponsored, authorized, endorsed, or approved this book.

Always read all information provided by the manufacturers' product labels before using their products. The author and publisher are not responsible for claims made by manufacturers.

Paperback Edition

Manufactured in the United States of America

DEDICATION

To all those persons who strive to find ways to simplify their life and to stop purchasing so many commercially made products I dedicate this book. It can be hard to get off the grid but with persistence and dedication you can do it.

TABLE OF CONTENTS

Publishers Notes 2

Dedication 3

Chapter 1- Homemade Soap Making 5

Chapter 2- The Benefits of Making Soap At Home 8

Chapter 3- Safety Precautions To Take When Making Soap At Home 11

Chapter 4- The Tools Required To Make Homemade Soap 14

Chapter 5- 10 Delightful Homemade Soap Recipes 17

Chapter 6- How To Make Your Own Laundry Detergent 39

About The Author 42

Chapter 1 - Homemade Soap Making

Interestingly enough, most people have been using soap since they were born, but the majority of people do not have the slightest clue how soap is made. Little do most people know, soap is actually salt that occurred from a chemical process. In some chemistry classes, they actually teach people how to make soap. However, an individual does not have to understand the chemical process just to make soap.

Soap is made from a process called saponification. The way it happens is through the chemical makeup. Soap will have a reaction from both an acid and a base. This reaction that occurs from both an acid and a base combined create the salt that we call soap.

Traditional Soap Making Techniques Explained

When it comes to soap making, the thing people have to understand is that they must consider the chemical makeup of both the acid and the base. When making soap, people mix oils and fats into lye in order to form the soap. Many different types of acids can be used to help saponify the base, and this is one of the reasons why soap-making has become somewhat of an interesting hobby and art. The acid could be olive oil, tallow or coconut oil. The ranges of acids that can be used are almost unlimited, but the unique combination will combine to the base and create something unique every time.

The one thing that every soap maker will tell people is that the acid needed will vary based on the chemical makeup of the acid. One of the remarkable things about soap making is that it allows an individual to create the type of soap that he/she wants. For example, some people might prefer the natural coloring of soap while others might use crayons in order to give the soap a specific color. With soap making, people can create a soap that is smooth, or they can add some herbs in order to give a texture to it. It depends on the needs and interests of the person who is making it. Some don't like the texture when it is put into it.

When it comes to soap making, the thing about it is that people can allow their imagination to run free. The more they imagine it, the more fun they will have, which means that they will enjoy it more. Sometimes people will put lavender flowers into soap and they end up turning black. This can look pretty ugly to some people, so a person has to know where his/her own individual preferences lie.

One of the greatest things about soap making is that it allows a person to create unique fragrances as well as soap. This hobby can even be turned into a small business as the person gets better at

Esther Beckett
making it. The best thing about soap making is the creativity and freedom that a person has with it.

Chapter 2 - The Benefits of Making Soap At Home

Making soap at home is one of the most exciting and exhilarating homemade products available, and can have a wonderful positive effect on the largest organ of the body, the skin. Producing your own soap can be a fun thing to do with family members, particularly when the correct safety steps are taken to ensure the combination of lye and water are handled correctly to avoid any burning of the skin. Amongst the benefits of making soap at home are the sense of achievement and the positive effects of producing real soap, not the mass produced detergents passed off as soaps in most retail stores.

The first major benefit of producing soap at home is the sense of achievement an individual or group gets when a small amount of soap can be seen sitting on the surface of water as lye, water and oils are mixed together during the soap production process. Making homemade soap can be time consuming, but offers a real sense of achieving something when a natural bar of soap can be used in the shower or bath.

Most people set out on the journey to create their own soap when they read about the removal of glycerine from the majority of soap bars in the 21st century. By making soap at home, glycerine the chemical produced during the soap making process that aids in lathering and moisturizing the skin, is maintained in the homemade soap. Many manufacturers of bar soaps remove the glycerine from their products and preserve it for use in lotions and moisturizers designed to replace the moisture removed by using mass produced bar soap detergents.

Many consumers become concerned about the type of ingredients included in mass produced bar soaps, with the process of creating soap at home being encouraged as the individual can then tailor make the soap with the ingredients of their own choosing. These ingredients can include natural products that are designed to detoxify the body or cater to the allergies an individual may have. One of the often included ingredients in homemade soaps is bentonite clay, which provides natural detoxification and is healthier for the skin.

People who have skin problems often feel the main benefit of producing their own soaps at home, which can be produced free from the many chemicals that are harsh to the skin over time. By producing a soap at home that is free of artificial chemicals, dyes and perfumes the problems of eczema and psoriasis can be reduced for those who have adverse effects to mass produced bar soaps.

Traditional Soap Making Techniques Explained

Finally, the main benefit of producing homemade soaps is that each and every bar is produced to the individual's personal requirements and is created to their own specifications. This can include a specific color or scent included to create the best soap available without the need for harsh chemicals and damaging materials.

Chapter 3- Safety Precautions To Take When Making Soap At Home

Making your own soap is fun and rewarding for you and your entire family. It is a hobby where you can learn new things as well as get creative, then enjoy the finished product. You probably do not immediately think of it as being a potentially dangerous hobby. But it actually is and this is thanks to one of the main ingredients: lye. It is a corrosive chemical that can damage your surfaces as well as burn you.

Before you get started making soap at home it is important that you understand all of the safety precautions. Despite the dangers, you should not be intimidated by homemade soap. As long as you follow all of the steps to stay safe and you are smart, you will be safe and the experience will be enjoyable.

A Distraction-Free Workspace

Pets and children can cause chaos. Chaos leads to rushing and forgetting steps. When you set up your soap-making workspace, be sure it is in a calm, quiet area of your home. This allows you to completely focus on your ingredients.

Organize

After establishing a workspace, make sure that everything you need for your batch of soap is there and ready. Soap-making involves a lot of timing and you do not want to find that something is missing when you need it, and then have to rush and find it. If you have everything on hand and accessible, you will cut out a lot of risk factors. Make sure everything is labelled as well, so you do not accidentally grab the wrong ingredient.

Measure Correctly

When doing any measurements for soap-making you should be using weight measurements not volume. This means you are using ounces and grams not cups or tablespoons. Invest in a quality digital scale because measurements need to be accurate.

Consider Your Containers

You will be working with lye. There are some materials that lye interacts with you and you need to avoid these. Instead, use thick glass, thick plastic or stainless steel. Also remember that your containers need to be heat-resistant. Materials that are not lye-safe include: Tin, Zinc and Aluminum.

Know How to Handle Lye

Because lye is both an important and dangerous ingredient, it is vital that you understand how to work with it. Only buy pure lye and be sure to wear safety goggles, rubber gloves and hard shoes. Avoid long sleeves and stick to rubber gloves that go farther up your arm. When mixing lye with other ingredients always pour the lye or the lye-solution into the other solution and never the other way around. This helps you to avoid splashing the lye. Always pour slowly and carefully. Vinegar will neutralize lye, so you should always have vinegar as part of your workspace in case of a spill.

Chapter 4 - The Tools Required To Make Homemade Soap

Humans have been making homemade soap for thousands of years. As a matter of fact, evidence of a soap-like substance has been discovered and dated to approximately 2800 BC. Of course historically, homemade soap was a matter of necessity rather than choice. Today, many people choose to return to the homemade method of soap-making to gain control of the chemicals introduced to their bodies as well as enjoying the art. There are several tools you will need to successfully make your own brand of homemade soap.

Safety Equipment

Safety is primary. As mentioned in Chapter 3, never attempt to make soap without appropriate eye-goggles and rubber gloves. Do not skimp on the quality of these products. The lye used in making soap is extremely caustic and can cause serious eye and skin injury.

Containers And Utensils

Many of these tools are commonly found in your kitchen. However, only use tools dedicated to soap-making. One large heat-resistant pitcher for mixing and pouring the lye solution. Two large stainless steel pots, one for combining lye with oils and the second pot for heating oils, fats and additives. Several wooden or silicone spoons and spatulas for mixing and pouring the ingredients. Wooden utensils will need to be replaced more frequently as the chemicals degrade the wood. A hand held mixer or an immersion blender will also be needed. Using an immersion blender will reduce the time it takes to saponify (the chemical reaction between the oils, fats and lye) the soap.

Scale

Esther Beckett

To ensure a proper chemical reaction between your ingredients, an accurate scale is essential to measure lye, oils, fats and other additives in your soap recipe. Look for a scale capable of measuring 1/10 of an ounce.

<u>Thermometer</u>

Two quick-reading thermometers are needed for the soap-making process. One is used for measuring the temperature of the lye and the other for oil and fats.

<u>Molds And Cutters</u>

A wide variety of different molds are available for homemade soap-making. Manufactured molds are frequently made from a silicone based product or wood. Whether you choose to form your soap into a basic bar shape or create unique guest-soaps, there is probably a mold available to fit your desire. If you are feeling especially creative, you may choose to design and make your own mold. Perhaps you prefer a more rustic look. If so, a soap-cutter may be your tool of choice. Soap is poured into a tray and the cutter blade is used to slice the soap. Miter boxes are available to ensure uniform slices if desired.

<u>Recipe</u>

Soap-making is not only an art form, it is a scientific equation. Beginning soap-makers should use a tried and true recipe. Hobby stores, the library and the Internet are all valuable resources for recipes and techniques. This list represents the basic tools needed for a beginning soap-maker. As your skills and creativity increase, you may find the need and desire to expand on these basic instruments. Whether you are looking for carving tools or packaging for your finished product, there is a multitude of offerings available. Have fun and be safe.

Chapter 5 - 10 Delightful Homemade Soap Recipes

Simple Handmade Soap

Soap can be a fun and easy way to cut costs. This homemade soap recipe is great for pregnant women with concerns about all the dye and unnatural ingredients that can come with store bought brands. To make your own soap at home you will first need to obtain the following ingredients:

- 50 g unprocessed Shea butter
- 150 g coconut butter
- 50 g cocoa butter
- 50 g palm butter
- 45 g castor oil
- 61.5 g sodium hydroxide
- 160.50 ml distilled water
- 150 g olive oil

In addition to the ingredients there are numerous tools that are needed in making soap from home. The following are required for cold processed soap:

- A scale is needed for measuring the two butters and sodium hydroxide
- Glass bowl for combining distilled water and sodium hydroxide
- A measuring cup for the oils
- A stainless steel pan for warming the butters and oils
- Both a glass and wood spoon
- Plastic shapes to pour the soap paste in them
- A spoon for mixing, preferably glass.
- Mixer

Traditional Soap Making Techniques Explained

- A knife for cutting the soaps
- Two thermometers (glass)

This solid soap recipe is made using the cold process. Below you can find step by step instructions on the process of making cold processed soap.

- First you weigh the sodium hydroxide, the distilled waters, oils and butters with the scale.
- You then mix the water with the sodium hydroxide by pouring the sodium hydroxide over the water, a little at a time until fully dissolved. The goal temperature for this is between 33 and 43°C.
- The oil mixture has the target temperate of 33 and 43°C.
- When the mixture has reached the optimal temperature, pour the water/sodium hydroxide mixture, over oil mixture. Mix it with the glass stick until they are slowly blended.

- Continue the blending with a mixer until the mixture leave a trace. Leaving a trace means that when you remove the mixer from the bowl, the composition leaves a soap trace on top of the mixer.

- Now is the step where you add the scented oils of your choice and continue mixing until fully blended. By mixing the list of oils below you will create a soothing and gentle smell perfect for pregnancy:

    - 10 ml lavender essential oil
    - 5 ml lemon essential oil
    - 15 ml sweet almond oil

- Slowly pour the soap into the plastic shapes with a ladle. Using the glass spoon continue to slowly mix the soap after you pour them in shapes.
- Then cover your soap molds with a towel and leave them for 24 hours. After 24 hours take the soaps out of the shapes and enjoy!

This recipe creates a sudsy lather that is perfect for anyone but especially a pregnant woman. The lack of chemicals and artificial ingredients is great for sensitive skin and the simple instructions are easy to follow.

Homemade Lye Soap

Ingredients

- 2 lbs. fat. (You have a choice between lard, tallow or organic palm oil).
- Distilled water.

Traditional Soap Making Techniques Explained

- Lye (Please note that the amount of lye you need will vary depending on the type of fat you use. Using a lye calculator will help determine the right amount).

There are two methods for making this soap; the hot method and cold method. The hot method is discussed below.

Steps

- First you will measure the lye and the water, each in different bowls.
- Combine the water and lye by carefully pouring the lye into the water. (It is important to note that pouring the water into the lye should be avoided).
- Next, mix and stir until the lye is all the way dissolved. Take care not to touch the mixture as it is corrosive and can damage your skin. Also, be aware that the bowl is going to be very hot.
- Place the bowl under a vent or other cooling device, to allow the bowl to cool while you ready the fats or oils.
- Melt the fats or oils on low heat until they are melted.
- When they are melted, add the water/lye mix to the melted fat or oil and stir. Also, be sure to decontaminate anything the lye touches with soap, water and white vinegar mixed together.
- Blend the lye mixture and the oils/fats together for an additional 5 minutes until the mixture becomes thick, similar to pudding.
- When the mixture is the right consistency, place the mixture back onto your heat source and allow 1 hour for the mixture to cook.

- While you are waiting for the mixture to cook, grab a mold and line it with parchment paper or a similar non-stick substance.
- After the soap is finished cooking you can either pour it into your mold or use a spoon for greater control.
- The soap then needs to cool for an additional 24 hours until it has hardened.
- When the soap has hardened, remove the soap from your mold and cut it into pieces or bars.
- Next, place the bars onto a tray to cool even more, but you can use your first bar right away if you like.
- This soap can also be used in your laundry or dish detergent if shredded, so feel free to use the soap in this way if you like.

There you have it; the recipe to make lye soap. This soap may also help with poison ivy, poison oak, poison sumac and bug bites. Also, please note that this soap may dry out your skin with everyday use. However, it is great for those with more oily skin.

Spice And Coffee Soap

Cleanliness is next to Godliness. That's what my mother used to say. As an adult and a parent, I now see the wisdom in those words. But does that mean that I have to bathe with the same old boring soap? Not at all. There are many different types of soap that you can make yourself at home. This is a recipe for homemade Spice and Coffee Soap.

Base Oils

- 10 oz. coconut oil
- 12 oz. olive oil
- 2 oz. castor oil

Traditional Soap Making Techniques Explained

- 6 oz. palm oil-sustainable
- Optional: 1/2 oz. Jojoba oil

<u>Lye Solution</u>

- 10 oz. cooled coffee- triple strength
- 4.30 oz. lye with 6% excess fat

<u>Exfoliant</u>

- 2 or 3 Tbsp. wet or dry coffee grounds

<u>Add-Ins</u>

- 1 tsp. cloves-ground
- 1 tbsp. cinnamon-ground
- 1 tsp. cloves-ground
- 2 oz. your choice of essential oils

<u>Steps</u>

- Using distilled water, brew coffee. Place in refrigerator for 3 hours or overnight.
- Measure the coffee and the lye into separate containers. Measure these with a kitchen scale. Use a lye calculator to assure that the amounts of lye, liquid, and oils are used.
- Add the lye to the coffee and dissolve completely. Do not touch this liquid. Beware that the bowl will become hot. Lye is a dangerous product to work with and extreme caution should be used. Follow all package directions completely.
- Place the mixture under a vent to allow it to cool off.

- Weigh out the oils (except the Jojoba oil-that will be added later) that you will use and melt them in a crock-pot on low.
- After melted, add the coffee/lye to the crock-pot, stir. Note: All utensils need to be cleaned with white vinegar, soap, and water after using to neutralize the lye.
- Using a hand held blender, combine oils and crock-pot contents for 1-2 minutes, until the mixture reaches the "trace" stage.
- Add in the cinnamon, cloves, ginger, and coffee grounds and blend for 2-3 minutes until the mix is a pudding consistency.
- Cover and "cook" on low for 1 hour.
- Prepare the mold for your soap.
- Remove the lye mixture from the heat. Quickly add the essential oils and stir until combined.
- Use a spoon to fill soap molds or pour into mold.
- Allow 24 hours for soap to cool and harden.
- Turn out the soap onto cutting board. Cut into preferred size bars.
- Lay out bars on rack for further cooling and hardening. You can use one immediately if preferred.

When it is time to scrub up after a hard day's work, there is nothing better than cleaning up with your own hand made scented exfoliating soap made with spices and coffee. This soap is sure to leave your skin clean, smooth, and you choose the scent.

Homemade Fruit Soap

Homemade fruit soap is simple and easy to make. The best part of using homemade fruit soap is that you know all the ingredients that went into it, so you control what goes on your skin! Making soap at home is an activity that can be done as a family as well.

Materials

- Rubbing alcohol
- Dry, clean containers such as Tupperware or margarine containers to use as a mold for the soap
- Vegetable oil cooking spray or Vaseline
- Glycerin soap base
- Paring knife
- Heat resistant glass measuring cup

Ingredients

These ingredients are based on what fruits you would like to use in your soap. The following ingredients are recommendations.

- 1 lemon peel
- 1 orange peel
- 1/3 cup of blueberries
- 1/3 cup of strawberries

Steps

- Wash and dry all citrus peels and berries. Separate the fruits and puree each individually. The fruit should be moist enough on its own to puree but if it is not, add 1tsp of water to the mixture and puree. Bear in mind that you do not want the fruit to be overly moist. Once done, place the purees to the side.
- Pour water into the mold. Pour this water into your measuring cup and note the amount of water you poured in. Discard the water and be sure to dry the mold entirely.

This amount of water used in the mold will determine how much glycerin soap base you will need to melt for the mold

- Coat your mold with either the cooking spray or Vaseline, whichever you plan on using. Be sure to coat evenly and wipe out any excess that may be left.
- Next want to chop the glycerin soap base into chunks. Cutting into smaller chunks is best. Place these chunks in your glass measuring cup and microwave. Be sure that the glycerin soap base is melted. Add more glycerin soap base as needed until you reach the amount of water you measured in earlier steps. Once melted, stir the glycerin soap base until it is smooth.
- Next measure out the fruit puree per cup of soap. Each cup of soap will receive 1 teaspoon of puree per cup of soap. Stir the fruit puree into the soap mixture to keep from sinking to the bottom. Add more fruit puree if desired. Mix and match your fruits as you prefer. Heavier pieces of fruit will sink to the bottom while lighter pieces will be at the top. Once the soap has cooled but is not solid, pour into mold.
- Be sure to pour about ¾ of an inch of soap in each mold. Spraying the surface with rubbing alcohol will help to eliminate any bubbles that may form. Leave soap out about a half hour before moving to your freezer for two hours.
- Pry soap out of container after being in the freezer. Use as desired!

Herb-Based Handmade Soap

Making homemade soap and infusing it with herbs is a great way to make it more beneficial for your skin. There are numerous kinds of herbs out there that you can use for soap such as Calendula, which

Traditional Soap Making Techniques Explained

helps to sooth inflamed skin and rashes while also helping to reduce scars. There's also marshmallow root which soothes, lubricates, and softens skin.

<u>Ingredients</u>

- 1 ounce of Shea butter
- 1 cup of calendula petals
- 13.5 ounces of water
- 18.5 ounces of olive oil
- 3 tablespoons of essential oils
- Half a cup of marshmallow root
- 5.8 ounces of powdered lye (also known as Sodium Hydroxide)
- 9 ounces of Palm oil
- 12 ounces of coconut oil

<u>Materials</u>

- A mesh strainer
- A quart-sized Mason jar (or something similar to put the soap in)
- Gloves
- A stainless steel pot
- An immersion blender
- Soap Molds (Can be a bread loaf pan)
- Several heat-resistant bowls
- A digital scale
- Freezer paper

<u>Steps</u>

- You want to start by putting the calendula petals in a quart-sized jar while filling the rest of the jar with boiling water. Let it set over night.
- Strain the infused water using the mesh strainer and put into another jar.
- Turn the oven on to 200 degrees Fahrenheit and then turn it off once it's heated.
- Add the olive oil, 1/4 of the marshmallow root, and 1/4 of the calendula petals into a heat-resistant bowl and place in the oven.
- In another bowl mix the coconut oil, 1/4 of the marshmallow root, and 1/4 of the calendula petals. You can melt the coconut oil beforehand but it will melt in the oven.
- Leave both bowls in the oven for approximately 4 hours.
- Strain each infused oil using the mesh strainer into their own jars. Do not mix.
- Place the stainless pot on the scale and starting pouring in the infused olive oil until the scale reaches the required weight of this recipe. Then tare the scale.
- Next, add the infused coconut oil to the scale until it reaches the required weight of this recipe and then tare the scale.
- Finally, add the required amounts of the palm oil and Shea butter to the mix.
- Place the stainless pot on the stove, but don't turn it on until you've stirred the lye and water in. While adding the lye, be careful not to get it on yourself.
- While you wait for that, you can start lining your soap molds with the freezer paper.
- You'll want to pour the lye into a bowl of water, taking note that as mentioned in Chapter 3, it can't be done the

other way around. Then stir. Cool down the lye and all the oils to 110 degrees Fahrenheit.
- You can then mix them using the immersion blender and then pour the blend into the soap molds and keep 48 hours.

Coconut Oil Soap

Creating your own handmade coconut oil soap can be fun; however, you must take safety precautions since you will work with lye. The ingredients are simple to locate (you can find 100% lye at hardware store in the drain cleaning section). Keep in mind that lye can be dangerous and may cause burns.

The equipment used should be used specifically for soap making, not for cooking food. You need an 8-quart crock pot, measuring cups and bowls (glass is best), spoons and a spatula. A stick blender works great for mixing because it reaches inside pots and bowls. Also needed is a digital scale and thermometer. You can use soap molds or a bread baking pan (just be sure to line the molds with parchment paper first).

Place a bowl full of vinegar and water to clean items coming in contact with the lye; this should be followed by a soap and water cleaning. Use some protective eyewear and rubber gloves.

Ingredients

- Bottle of lye
- 4.83 ounces for soap
- coconut oil - 33 ounces at 76 degrees Fahrenheit
- water - 12 and one half ounces
- essential oils (five to one ounce)

Steps

- Make sure you weigh all the ingredients.
- Put the crockpot on a low setting.
- Add water to a medium-sized glass or bowl and take it outside (or a well-ventilated area) along with the lye and long-handled spoon.
- Add lye to the water and stir it gently (use protective eye wear when you are working with the lye).
- Be sure to mix water and lye in a space that is open and nicely ventilated since lye's fumes can be dangerous if inhaled. This mixture will be extremely hot. You will then see the mixture change from one that is cloudy to clear. Let this cool for about 15 minutes.
- Next you are ready to put the coconut oil inside a pan and heat it.
- Take your crockpot and place the heated coconut oil and lye inside. Stir this gently, adding care not to splash.
- Begin mixing this using the stick blender. Mix until a lightweight pudding texture is achieved. With the cover on allow this to cook about one hour.

The hardest thing with soap making is determining if it is ready. If it is, it will resemble the look of Vaseline, exempt from oil patches. To test for doneness take a bit of soap and rub it around your fingers. You want this to feel like wax. You can also perform a trace test by placing a drop of the soap to the upper pot surface. If the soap drop remains on the surface it is ready but if it sinks back in the pot, it is not. Place the mixture in the mold and let cool. Add essential oils.

Citrus And Herb Soap

Ingredients

Traditional Soap Making Techniques Explained

- Your choice of citrus fruit (Grapefruits, Limes, or Lemons)
- Your choice of fresh herbs (rosemary, basil, and mint)
- Glycerin (can be bought at your local drug store such as Walgreens or CVS) to melt and pour your soap
- A food processor
- A soap mold, clean yogurt container, or small glass bowl (soap mold is preferred; however it can be replaced with one of the other items if you don't have one.)

<u>Steps</u>

- Gather your supplies into one area in front of you so you are sure you have all of the ingredients you will need to make the soap. This also makes the process easier because you have everything there and you do not have to go around looking for supplies.
- Wash your fruit peels before you begin.
- Make sure they are totally dry before going any further with this recipe. The peels must be dry in order for the soap to come out correctly.
- Begin with the rind of your fruit. Wash it good and grind it until you cannot grind it anymore.
- Make your herbs into tiny pieces by using your food processor. If you are using rosemary you will have to mince it by hand.
- Make sure you do not combine the herbs and the citrus rind.
- You should keep them in separate piles. You will combine them later.
- Melt 1/2 cup of glycerin in the microwave.
- You want to mix in 1 teaspoon of the herbs and 1 teaspoon of the citrus next. Be sure this combination is mixed very well. This is what will become your soap so the citrus and

- herbs must be distributed as evenly as possible throughout the glycerin mixture.
- Now you should pour your mixture into a soap mold if you have one. Yogurt containers that are totally and completely washed out and clean small glass bowls work fine as replacements, however if you are using one of these you should cover it in a thin layer of vegetable oil before adding the mixture so that your soap does not stick. If you have a soap mold it is recommended that you use it. Soap molds are pliable so the soap comes out a lot easier.
- Finally, let your soap sit in the mold at room temperature for 60 minutes. Leave the soap undisturbed.
- Once that time is up, put it into your freezer for another 20 minutes.
- Then remove your soap from your mold or container. If you happen to be using glass bowl or yogurt containers, you may have to loosen the edges of the soap with a butter knife in order for it to fall out of the container.
- Then it is time to relax and enjoy the soap you made.

Olive Oil Soap

Originating from the Castile region of Spain, olive oil soap is known for possessing gentle moisturizing capabilities. This soap can be found in stores but is often expensive or full of harsh chemicals. Fortunately, one can easily make it themselves in their own home for a fraction of the price. Using the simple recipe below it won't be long till there is an abundant amount of environmentally friendly soap in your home.

Oil

- 567 grams olive oil

Traditional Soap Making Techniques Explained

<u>Lye mixture</u>

- 73 grams sodium hydroxide (NaOH)
- 215 grams distilled water

<u>Equipment</u>

- Measuring cups
- An empty jug
- A funnel
- A stick blender
- Large metal pot (not aluminum!)
- Goggles
- Plastic apron
- Rubber gloves

<u>Steps</u>

- Put on the gloves, rubber apron, and goggles.
- Go to a well-ventilated area with the lye and the water. Pour the measured water into the empty jug. Place a funnel at the top and slowly add the lye to the water.
- Cap the jug. Lightly swish the mixture around for a few moments. Uncap the jug to release the buildup of gasses.
- Measure the olive oil in a measuring cup and then pour into the metal pot.
- Heat olive oil to 110 degrees Fahrenheit. Remove from heat immediately.
- Temperature check the lye-water, wait until it cools down to 110 degrees Fahrenheit.
- Slowly pour the lye water into the pot with the oil.

- With the stick blender stir in a figure eight pattern until the mixture is thick enough to leave a trail. The blender should not be continuously on but pulsed on and off throughout this period of time.
- Pour into the desired mold. Be sure to have lined it with wax paper before use to insure an easy extraction once the soap has cured.
- The soap then needs to rest in the mold for at least 48 hours. Olive oil soap can take a little longer to cure than most soaps and will need at least 4 to 6 weeks to fully cure. Once ready, take it out of the mold and enjoy!

Lye Safety

Lye is highly toxic and needs to be handled with care to reduce the chances of accidents. The body must always be fully covered with a rubber apron, gloves, and eye goggles. One must always add lye to water and not the other way around. If one were to pour water into lye the mixture would explode, sending lye and water all over the area.

It is also important to keep a bottle of white vinegar around to use in case of spills. Vinegar is an acid and will neutralize lye when put into contact with it. If lye is spilled on a person or a surface pour vinegar on it first before cleaning it up.

Refreshing Mint Soap

Mint soap can be so incredibly refreshing. Not only does that amazing tingling sensation from fresh mint soap revive and cool your skin during the warm summer months, but it is a wonderfully relaxing aromatherapy when it is combined with the steam from a hot shower as well.

Traditional Soap Making Techniques Explained

While many boutiques and specialty shops will sell a variety of mint soaps at a premium, a number of homemade variations are available that won't drain the bank. Unknown to many, you do not need any dangerous special chemicals to make mint soap at home. The most efficient way to make your own mint soap is with the use of melt and pour soap bases.

A wonderful (and fairly inexpensive) gift for any holiday, homemade mint soap is simple to make. Now you can make and enjoy your own homemade mint soap with just a few simple ingredients, some common kitchen equipment, approximately 10 minutes prep time, and a little skill!

Ingredients

- Shea Butter Melt and Pour Type Soap Base (or other white or clear meltable soap base as desired)
- Peppermint Essential Oil or Spearmint Essential Oil
- Dried crushed mint leaves
- Red or Green Soap Colorant (optional)

Materials

- Soap Mold (Gelatin molds work great for a little creativity
- Microwave safe Measuring Cup (with optional pour spout for convenience)
- Toothpicks or a sharp knife

Steps

- Cut or break the melt and pour soap base into smaller pieces (about 1-2 inches) and place them into the microwave safe cup.

Esther Beckett

- Microwave on high for 30 seconds at a time, stirring between intervals, until the soap base is completely melted.
- Add 6-10 drops of the mint essential oil (depending on your scent preference).
- Stir the crushed mint leaves into the mixture. Be sure to stir the ingredients well to ensure uniformity.
- Pour the melted soap base into the mold of your choice.
- If you are concerned about the soap sticking to the mold, rub it with baby oil or spray lightly with cooking spray before you pour in the soap mixture. Be sure to work quickly, since some soap bases set up fairly rapidly.
- Dot the top of the soap mixture with tiny drops of red or green soap coloring (food coloring will also work if you find yourself in a pinch) and swirl the colorant with a toothpick or knife for the desired effect.
- Allow the soap to cool completely, and it removes from mold by gently flexing the sides of the mold.

Homemade mint soap will keep wonderfully if you are considering gifting. Simply wrap neatly in cellophane wrap and secure with clear tape and a pretty homemade tie or bow.

Goat Milk Soap

Ingredients

- 24 Ounces of Spring Water
- 17 Ounces of Sodium Hydroxide (powder lye)

Oils

- 32 Ounces of coconut oil
- 32 Ounces of Crisco Shortening

Traditional Soap Making Techniques Explained
- 32 Ounces of Canola Oil
- 16 Ounces of Lemon Juice
- 2.7 Ounces of Goat's Milk (powder form)
- 2 Ounces of Stearic Acid (powder form)

Essential Oils

- 2 Ounces of Tea Tree Oil
- 1 Ounce of Vitamin E
- 1 Ounce of Sweet Almond Oil

Equipment

- 1 Pair of Rubber Gloves
- 1 Pair Eye Protection
- 1 Hair Protection Gear
- 1 10x20 Wooden Boxes
- 1 8-quart Stainless Steel large Pot (deep)
- 1 Long Wooden or Stainless Steel Spoon
- ½ Ounce of Vinegar (to stop the lye from burning if it touches skin place in small spray bottle for easy access and use)
- 1 Digital Scale
- 1 Wire Whisk

It takes about 45 minutes to an hour to mix, but it takes up to three weeks to cure, before the lye is nonreactive and able to use on the skin. Also please note that vinegar spray will naturalized the lye to relieve any burning sensation if lye gets on your skin.

This mixture makes 25 bars of soap at 4 ounces per bar of soap

Steps

Esther Beckett
Soap making is very dangerous please proceed with caution while performing this task.

- Start of by gathering all material required, measure, and place to the side. This should be done in a well-ventilated area, because inhaled chemicals may cause an allergic reaction.
- Put on all of your protective gear for your head, eye, and hands.
- Add water into the pot, then lye, and stir up with long spoon or stick.
- Add oils: coconut oil, Crisco shortening (whisk to speed up process). The substance will start to heat up and turn a pinkish color.
- Add canola oil and lemon juice pour in slowly to not disturb the chemical bond.
- Add goat's milk (brightens skin) and stearic acid (makes soap harder and latter) (mix together and break up lumps before adding to mixture).
- Add essential oils: Tea Tree (good for skin irritates and boils), Vitamin E (look for the vegetable type), and sweet almond oil.
- Stir continuously, and look for tracing. Once mixture traces then line your wooden box with plastic for easy removal of soap.
- Then pour in the mixture, and allow mixture to sit for two to three hours, before you cut the soap in to desired length and width.
- Skim the top of the soap first to make it easier to make smoother cuts through the soap.
- Allow the soap to rest for two to three days, before you pull out the soap from the wooden box. The soap should be hard before you remove it from the wooden box.

Traditional Soap Making Techniques Explained

- Then put the soap into drying boxes with vents stacked and lines with newspaper for at least three weeks for curing.
- Finally test the soap on corner or tip of tongue to make sure the lye is nonreactive if it does not burn your tongue then it is ready to use. If your tongue starts to burn spray with vinegar and allow one more week for the soap to cure.

Please note you should always test the soap before use.

Chapter 6 - How To Make Your Own Laundry Detergent

With everyone looking to tighten their budgets in a dipping economy, it is becoming increasingly common for people to forget about buying expensive name brand products for the home. Instead, people are resorting to more "do it yourself" projects to save money and live a simpler life. This trend is catching on in many different aspects of home life. One method of saving on laundry has been particularly popular in the past few months. More and more people have begun making their own homemade laundry soap and detergent to ease the costs of the often expensive laundry detergents and soaps that are usually purchased.

This Chapter provides both a recipe for liquid detergent and powdered detergent; both are effective alternatives to these expensive household products.

Recipe For Liquid Detergent

Ingredients

Traditional Soap Making Techniques Explained

- 1/2 standard size bar of generic soap
- 3/4 cup borax powder
- 3/4 cup washing soda

<u>Steps</u>

- Use a cheese grater to grate up the bar of soap (this step could also be completed by adding the soap to a food processor).
- Next, add the grated soap to a large pot. Pour 9 cups of water into the pan.
- Heat the pot on medium heat and continue to heat until the soap has melted into the water and the mixture is smooth. Now, you can add the borax powder and the washing soap.
- Heat the concoction until the powders have dissolved and the ingredients have been thoroughly combined.
- Remove from the heat. Next, prepare a large bucket with a lid by adding 6 cups of hot water to the bottom.
- Add your soap and powder mixture to the bucket and stir the two together.
- Once combined, add another gallon and a half of water to the mixture and stir until thoroughly homogeneous.
- Seal the bucket. The soap will be runny for a day or so before it begins to gel together.

Use about 1/2 cup of the mixture per load of laundry and be sure to the keep the mixture sealed and store in a place of moderate temperature.

<u>Recipe For Powdered Detergent</u>

<u>Ingredients</u>

Esther Beckett

- 1 bar regular, generic bar soap
- 2 cup borax powder
- 2 cup washing soda

<u>Steps</u>

- Once again, begin the process by grating the bar soap and cutting it into fine pieces with a food processor. The soap should be in small enough pieces to be easily mixed in with the powders, so it should be processed quite well.
- Next, use a large bowl to combine the ingredients.
- Mix the powders well, ensuring they are well combined.
- Once all of the ingredients have been thoroughly incorporated, you can transfer the mixture to a large air-tight container.
- It is helpful to store the powdered detergent with a measure spoon or cup.
- You should use between a 1/8 and a 1/4 of a cup per load of laundry.

About The Author

Esther Beckett has been making homemade soap for years. It was a tradition that was passed down from her great-grandmother and she is passed it on to her children who have kept the tradition going. At first she started making homemade soap as a hobby and to have the ability to control what was in the product. After a while Esther found that she could make it into viable small business.

Over the years it has grown and she has also spent time educating others on the skills of making homemade soap. This eventually led to her writing books about the process.

www.ingramcontent.com/pod-product-compliance
Ingram Content Group UK Ltd.
Pitfield, Milton Keynes, MK11 3LW, UK
UKHW022218230426
12048UKWH00016BA/921

9 781633 830363